This book is about:

_____   _____
My English Name   *My Hebrew Name*

Who was born on:

_____   _____
Secular Date   *Hebrew Date*

place photo here

El-hanaar ha'zeh heetpahlalti.
אֶל־הַנַּעַר הַזֶּה הִתְפַּלָּלְתִּי.
For this child I have prayed.

I Samuel 1:27

Handprint:

Footprint:

This little child, may he/she grow big.
—from *The New Jewish Baby Book: Names, Ceremonies and Customs*—
A Guide for Today's Families, by Anita Diamant

THE NEW JEWISH BABY ALBUM

Creating and Celebrating the
Beginning of a Spiritual Life—

A Jewish Lights Companion

The Editors at Jewish Lights
Introduction by Anita Diamant
Preface by Rabbi Sandy Eisenberg Sasso

JEWISH LIGHTS Publishing
Woodstock, Vermont

The New Jewish Baby Album:
Creating and Celebrating the Beginning of a Spiritual Life—A Jewish Lights Companion

First Printing 2003

Thank you to all of our friends who helped make this book rich with creative spiritual content: Rabbi Nina Beth Cardin, Anita Diamant, Rabbi Daniel Judson, Rabbi Karyn Kedar, Karen Kushner, Rabbi Lawrence Kushner, Rabbi Noa Kushner, Rabbi Jeffrey Salkin, Rabbi Sandy Eisenberg Sasso, Elisheva S. Urbas—and most of all to Lauren Seidman of Jewish Lights Publishing who brought this from concept to completion, and to her new nephew, Samuel Agustin Martinez, who inspired her in the process. Thanks, too, to all of the Jewish Lights authors whose inspiring words are included here.

Library of Congress Cataloging-in-Publication Data
The new Jewish baby album : creating and celebrating the beginning of a spiritual life—a Jewish lights companion / by the editors at Jewish Lights ; introduction by Anita Diamant ; preface by Rabbi Sandy Eisenberg Sasso.
p. cm,
ISBN 1-58023-138-1
1. Jewish children—Religious life. 2. Baby books. 3. Judaism—Customs and practices.
4. Fasts and feasts—Judaism. I. Jewish Lights Publishing (Firm)
BM727.N49 2003
296.4'4—dc21
2002156549

Cover and text design and typesetting: Bridgett Taylor
Hebrew typesetting: Ronnie Serr, Alphabet House, Los Angeles
Title page art: Phoebe Stone, *In God's Name*

10 9 8 7 6 5 4 3 2 1

Manufactured in Hong Kong

Published by Jewish Lights Publishing
A Division of LongHill Partners, Inc.
Sunset Farm Offices, Route 4, P.O. Box 237
Woodstock, VT 05091
Tel: (802) 457-4000   Fax: (802) 457-4004
www.jewishlights.com

MELANIE HALL / IN OUR IMAGE

Contents

Children

Loving God,
what is more precious
than our children?
Is there any treasure that can be
more beloved,
more pure
than those cherished souls
we have brought into the world?
Help me guide them well,
dear God,
and help them accept my guidance.
Help them lead their lives
with faith,
wisdom
and truth.

—Rebbe Nachman of Breslov,
*The Gentle Weapon: Prayers for Everyday
and Not-So-Everyday Moments,* by Moshe Mykoff

PHOEBE STONE / *IN GOD'S NAME*

Introduction

Anita Diamant

A baby book is a time machine. What lies between the covers—the facts and photographs, the little details and momentous events—can transport people and permit them to relive the most awesome, miraculous, and (let's be honest) the most physically exhausting moments of life.

A baby book is not merely a diary. It is a record of wonders that can instantly sweep you right to the moment your little boy said "ball," to the day your little girl took her first step. And baby books are time-traveling portals not only for parents, but for children, too. "The Story of Me" is the most fascinating story you can tell a five-year-old. And then someday—far, far off in the future—when the five-year-old becomes a father or a mother, this same baby book will become an even more precious legacy of magic and memory.

What makes this baby album different from all other baby books?

For Jews, remembering is a sacred obligation. The rituals and holidays that infuse Jewish living and define Jewish time are attempts at stopping the relentless flow of time, in order to empower memory and permit us to reflect on the meaning of our days. What sets this book apart from all the other baby books is that it folds our personal mementos into the context of Jewish remembering, of Jewish history.

Thus your baby's first Passover is not simply an extremely cute photo opportunity (the frog-festooned bib! the first taste of *haroset!*); it's also a profoundly moving record of Jewish continuity—the newest branch on a genealogical tree with roots as ancient as Egypt, as mysterious as Sinai.

This baby book provides parents with words and frameworks to help express emotions and insights that ultimately defy language; the awe that children teach us every day; the underlying unity of all life. Using the great gifts of Judaism—life-cycle events, holidays, blessings—this book is a record of your family's place in the unfolding miracle of creation.

As a parent, you have become "a tree of life." It is up to you to begin recording this unique and precious chapter of that sacred story.

Preface

Rabbi Sandy Eisenberg Sasso

For even the most rational among us, the moment of birth is miraculous. More than a biological process reaching its culmination, it is a moment when dreams and hopes become a life. We hold a new creation in our arms, a baby so close to our hearts and yet separate from our selves. We marvel at all the features: hands and feet, in miniature size; and a soul, large enough to contain the imprint of the Divine.

Holding our child for the first time is sealed forever in memory. When we call forth this memory in years to come, there will still be a shiver that moves through our hearts. Our arms, a love cradle; our whispered prayer, a lullaby song. We marvel at the mystery of life, at God's presence enfolding us.

There will be many holidays together, many new foods to be tried, places to be visited, new words to speak, and steps to take for years to come. But the very first times are infinitely precious; they are how we draw the map of the soul.

Among the first keepsakes of our child's birth is the ink footprint taken at the hospital. As our child grows, many footprints will decorate our floors and many handprints will adorn our walls. With time, they will fade. But those first movements, smiles, and words will leave indelible imprints on our hearts.

In years to come, these pages will transport us back to those beginning days and months, the whirl of activity, the sleepless nights, and the wonder of small gestures and little milestones. To remember these gives immeasurable joy.

Barukh ata Adonay m'sameiach horim im yaldeihem.

בָּרוּךְ אַתָּה יְיָ, מְשַׂמֵּחַ הוֹרִים עִם יַלְדֵיהֶם.

Blessed is the Holy Source of Life who causes parents to rejoice with their children!

PHOEBE STONE / IN GOD'S NAME

Before I Was Born

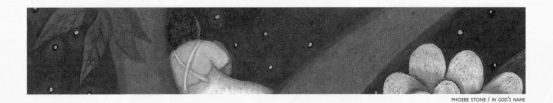

May you live to see your world fulfilled,
May your destiny be for worlds still to come,
And may you trust in generations past and yet to be.
May your heart be filled with intuition
and your words be filled with insight.
May songs of praise ever be upon your tongue
and your vision be on a straight path before you.
May your eyes shine with the brightness of the heavens.
May your lips speak wisdom
and your fulfillment be in righteousness
even as you ever yearn to hear the words
of the Holy Ancient One of Old.

Brachot 17a

Mom's Page
Thoughts from Mom Before I Was Born

I've written this special prayer to help me bring you safely into the world:

_____

_____

_____

These are my hopes, dreams, and prayers for you, my child, whose life has been granted to me to love and nurture:

_____

_____

_____

_____

Here's a picture of me, your mom, as a baby:

place photo here

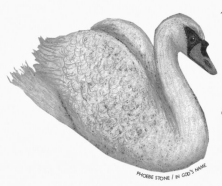

PHOEBE STONE / IN GOD'S NAME

The child to be born will depend on us as welcomers, nurturers, teachers and guides. God is entrusting a new child to our care, and we acknowledge our responsibility with appropriate awe, knowing that our strength to fulfill it also comes from God.

—Rick E. F. Dinitz and Tina D. Fein Dinitz, "A Holy Moment— Pregnant or Not," from _Lifecycles, Volume 1: Jewish Women on Life Passages & Personal Milestones_, edited by Rabbi Debra Orenstein

Dad's Page

Thoughts from Dad Before I Was Born

These are my hopes, dreams, and prayers for you, my child, whose life has been granted to me to love and nurture:

_____

_____

_____

_____

I've written this special prayer for my wife, your mom, to help her bring you safely into the world:

_____

_____

_____

Here's a picture of me, your dad, as a baby:

place photo here

As parents, we pray for our child's complete fulfillment.
May he or she have all the blessings we have had and more; may
he or she be blessed with gifts we have not yet imagined. As
God laughed when the rabbis surpassed even divine expecta-
tion, may we, too, laugh delightedly and say, "My children
have surpassed me. My children have surpassed me."

—Rabbi Debra Orenstein, *Lifecycles, Volume 1:*
Jewish Women on Life Passages & Personal Milestones

This is what Mom looked like pregnant:

place photo here

This is what I looked like inside of Mom:

ultrasound picture

Upon receiving this first glimpse of me, Mom and Dad felt:

_____

_____

_____

_____

_____

_____

_____

_____

Girls' names Mom and Dad liked:

_____

_____

_____

Boys' names Mom and Dad liked:

_____

_____

PHOEBE STONE / IN GOD'S NAME

Three partners create a child—the Holy One, the father and the mother.

BT *Niddah* 31A

My Family Tree

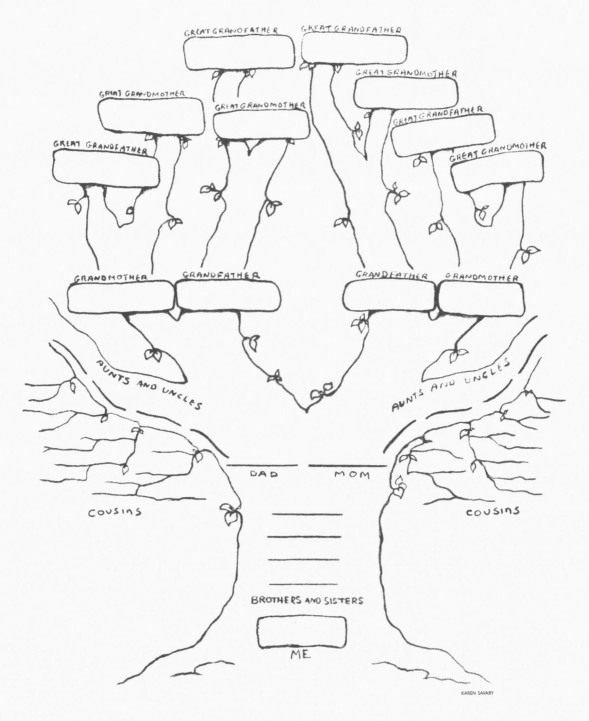

Just as our parents planted for us, so must we plant for our children.

Midrash Tanhuma Kedoshim 8

In every birth, blessed is the wonder
In every creation, blessed is the new beginning
In every child, blessed is life.
In every hope, blessed is the potential.
In every transition, blessed is the beginning.
In every existence, blessed are the possibilities
In every love, blessed are the tears.
In every life, blessed is the love.

—from *The New Jewish Baby Book:*
Names, Ceremonies and Customs—
A Guide for Today's Families, by Anita Diamant

PHOEBE STONE / *IN GOD'S NAME*

The Day of My Birth

Barukh ata Adonay Eloheynu melekh ha'olam she'hecheyanu v'kiy'manu v'higiyanu la'zman ha'zeh.

בָּרוּךְ אַתָּה, יְיָ אֱלֹהֵינוּ, מֶלֶךְ הָעוֹלָם,
שֶׁהֶחֱיָנוּ וְקִיְּמָנוּ וְהִגִּיעָנוּ לַזְּמַן הַזֶּה.

Blessed are You, Adonai, Ruler of Creation, who has kept us in life, sustained us, and enabled us to reach this season.

Barukh ata Adonay Eloheynu melekh ha'olam, hatov v'hameitiv.

בָּרוּךְ אַתָּה, יְיָ אֱלֹהֵינוּ, מֶלֶךְ הָעוֹלָם, הַטּוֹב וְהַמֵּטִיב.

Blessed are You, Adonai, Ruler of Creation, Who is good and does good.

PHOEBE STONE / *IN GOD'S NAME*

With each child, the world begins anew.

Midrash

I was born on _____

at _____ in _____.

I weighed _____ pounds and _____ ounces and was _____ inches long.

My head circumference was _____ inches, my eyes _____ and

my hair _____.

These people were present for my birth:

_____

_____

When they first met me, this is what my parents thought, felt, said or did:

_____

_____

_____

_____

_____

_____

_____

_____

There was a time when the world began. Having witnessed
a birth, parents seem to find that notion a bit less implau-
sible…. A midwife I interviewed told me, "Every time I
assist a mother giving birth, I always prepare her in advance.
I share with her my belief that at the instant she looks into
the face of her newborn child for the first time, just for
that second, she will see the face of God."

—Rabbi Nancy Fuchs-Kreimer, *Parenting As a Spiritual Journey:*
Deepening Ordinary & Extraordinary Events
into Sacred Occasions

MELANIE HALL / IN OUR IMAGE

The Torah portion for the week of my birth was _____
and my parents thought this part of it was especially meaningful for my life:

_____

_____

_____

On the day I was born the weather was _____.

The headlines were _____

_____

These were some important events in the Jewish world the week of my birth:

_____

_____

My grandparents and other relatives were very excited to meet me too, and these
were their wishes for me: _____

_____

_____

_____

_____

Parents discover in the ordinary and extraordinary moments
of their lives the reality of the unseen, the power beyond
words, the place where it all comes together.
And how they learn to "speak" about that reality
through a language beyond language:
through rituals and customs and deeds,
through metaphors and stories and prayers.

—Rabbi Nancy Fuchs-Kreimer,
Parenting As a Spiritual Journey:
Deepening Ordinary & Extraordinary Events
into Sacred Occasions

MELANIE HALL | IN OUR IMAGE

I came home on _____ and the first thing I did was _____.
Date

I was wearing _____ and the weather was _____.

My parents hung a mezuzah on the doorframe of my room on _____ and
Date

included Jewish decorations on my walls.... Here's a picture of my first room!

place photo here

The ... woman who nursed her newborn ... called God
Mother. The ... man who held the hand of his baby ... called
God *Father.*

—Rabbi Sandy Eisenberg Sasso, *In God's Name*

MELANIE HALL / *IN OUR IMAGE*

Our hearts are filled with delight and thankfulness on this day that we bring
a new precious life into our home. We will raise our child with love and
teach this child the values that have sustained the Jewish people for so
many centuries. May we never forget how blessed we feel today; may our
baby grow up happy and healthy.

—Lauren Seidman

16

Ceremonies & Celebrations

You stand this day, all of you, before your God—your tribal heads, your elders and your officials, all the men of Israel, your children, your wives, even the stranger within your camp, from the woodchopper to water-drawer—to enter into the covenant of your God, which your God is concluding with you this day, with its sanctions; to the end that God may establish you this day as God's people and be your God, as God promised you and as God swore to your fathers, Abraham, Isaac, and Jacob. I make this covenant, with its sanctions, not with you alone, but both with those who are standing here with us this day before God and with those who are not with us this day.

Deuteronomy 29:9–13

As you light your candles, so may your child's eyes be illuminated by Torah, by the wisdom of the world, by nature, and by people.

—from The Book of Jewish Sacred Practices:
CLAL's Guide to Everyday & Holiday Rituals & Blessings,
edited by Rabbi Irwin Kula and Vanessa L. Ochs, Ph.D.

MELANIE HALL / IN OUR IMAGE

Shalom Zachor/Shalom Nekaveh
Welcoming the Boy/Welcoming the Girl

We had a party on _____ to celebrate my first Shabbat at home (or one of
the first)!
Date

My grandparents or other relatives had these special blessings for me:

_____

_____

_____

_____

_____

Family, friends, and other guests had these special blessings for me:

_____

_____

_____

_____

_____

_____

Barukh ata Adonay Eloheynu melekh ha'olam, hagomel l'chayavim tovot,
shehg'malani kol tov.

בָּרוּךְ אַתָּה, יְיָ אֱלֹהֵינוּ, מֶלֶךְ הָעוֹלָם,
הַגּוֹמֵל לְחַיָּבִים טוֹבוֹת, שֶׁגְּמָלַנִי כָּל טוֹב.

Blessed are You, Adonai, Ruler of All, Who does good to the undeserving
and Who has dealt kindly with me.

Mi shehg'malcha kol tov, hu yigmolcha kol tov, selah.

מִי שֶׁגְּמָלְךָ כָּל טוֹב, הוּא יִגְמָלְךָ כָּל טוֹב, סֶלָה.

AVI KATZ / THE JEWISH FAMILY FUN BOOK

May the One Who has shown you kindness deal kindly with you forever.

Brit Bat
Covenant for a Daughter

For some people, holding a welcoming ceremony for their daughter marks the transition from individual baby into covenanted Jew…. The very notion of welcoming daughters in a religiously significant way is rooted in an egalitarian concept of what Judaism should be: different, perhaps, for females and males, but equal nonetheless.

—Debra Nussbaum Cohen, *Celebrating Your New Jewish Daughter: Creating Jewish Ways to Welcome Baby Girls into the Covenant*

May God Who blessed our mothers Sarah, Rebecca, Rachel, and Leah, Miriam the prophet and Avigayil, bless this beautiful little girl and let her name be called in Israel _____ daughter of _____
<small>My Hebrew Name</small> <small>Mom's Hebrew Name</small>
and _____ at this favorable moment of blessing. May she be
<small>Dad's Hebrew Name</small>
raised in health, peace, and tranquility to study Torah, to stand under the *chupah* (if that is her choice), and to do good deeds.

May God bless you and protect you.

May God's presence shine for you and be favorable to you.

May God's face turn to you and give you peace.

This blessing was said for me by _____.

I was named after _____ because
<small>Namesake/Relationship</small>
_____ and the name means
<small>Description of Namesake's Qualities</small>
_____.

She sits as a queen on a throne in Paradise, and the heavenly chambers are filled with her voice.

—Rabbi Sandy Eisenberg Sasso,
"A Psalm of Serach," in *But God Remembered: Stories of Women from Creation to the Promised Land*

BRIDGETT TAYLOR

Brit Milah
The Covenant of Circumcision

The covenant of circumcision is the oldest continuous Jewish rite, a ritual that unites Jews throughout ages and across cultures, and signifies the connection between individual human life and the Holy. With this ancient ceremony, parents announce their commitment to taking on the responsibilities and joys of raising a child according to the terms of the contract between God and the Jews.

—Anita Diamant, *The New Jewish Baby Book:*
Names, Ceremonies and Customs—A Guide for Today's Families

May this little child, _____ son of _____ and
$\qquad$ My Hebrew Name $\qquad$ Mom's Hebrew Name
_____, grow into manhood as a blessing to his family, the Jewish
Dad's Hebrew Name
people, and humanity. As he has entered the covenant of our people, so may

he grow into a life of Torah, *chupah* (if that is his choice), and good deeds.

May God bless you and keep you.

May God be with you and be gracious to you.

May God show you kindness and give you peace.

This blessing was said for me by _____.

I was named after _____ because
Namesake/Relationship
_____ and the name means
Description of Namesake's Qualities

_____.

There she saw a baby boy [Moses], more beautiful than any she had ever seen.

—Rabbi Sandy Eisenberg Sasso, "Bityah, Daughter of God," in
But God Remembered: Stories of Women from Creation to the Promised Land

Certificate of
Brit Bat/Brit Milah

My *Brit Bat / Brit Milah* was held on _____ at
                                      Hebrew Date/English Date

_____. _____ was the *sandek*.
Location   *Honored Guest Who Held Me*

My *kvatterin* is _____ and *kvatter* is _____.
                 Godmother   *Godfather*

Other guests were

_____

_____

_____

and they participated by

_____

_____

Rabbi: _____ Cantor: _____

Their special blessings for me:

_____

_____

_____

_____

_____

_____

Pidyon HaBen/Pidyon HaBat
Redemption of the Firstborn Child

The arrival of the firstborn child is a singular experience, deserving of its own ceremony. It is a time to celebrate a new Jewish life, and a new Jewish family.

Traditionally, firstborn sons who were not *Kohanim* (of the priestly caste) were obligated to serve the priesthood. The ritual of *Pidyon HaBen* was held on the thirty-first day of the baby boy's life, when his father would give five shekels of silver to the *Kohen*, or priest, as a substitute for giving up his son.

Modern *Pidyon HaBen* and *Pidyon HaBat* ceremonies take place on the one-month birthday of firstborn baby boys and girls. Instead of focusing on the redemption from priestly service, it honors the special gift of a first child. Rather than exchanging money to a *Kohen*, the family often gives *tzedakah* (charity) in the child's name, affirming their dedication to raising the child in a Jewish home.

My *Pidyon HaBen/Pidyon HaBat* was held on _____
Hebrew Date/English Date

at _____. *Tzedakah* in my name was given to _____.
Location

Guests included

_____

_____
Attach a Complete List

> This *tzedakah* instead of greed,
> This gift in place of selfishness,
> This commitment because of the blessing of a new life.
>
> —Rabbi Sandy Eisenberg Sasso, in *The New Jewish Baby Book:
> Names, Ceremonies and Customs—A Guide for Today's Families*, by Anita Diamant

This blessing was said for me by: _____.

JOANI KELLER ROTHENBERG / *CAIN AND ABEL*

Firsts & Favorites

The Rabbis tell us that we should attempt to say one hundred blessings a day. By encouraging us to do so, they are teaching us a profound lesson. One hundred times a day we should be alert to the wonders of life around us.

—Rabbi Nina Beth Cardin, "Blessings throughout the Day,"
from *The Rituals & Practices of a Jewish Life:
A Handbook for Personal Spiritual Renewal*,
edited by Rabbi Kerry M. Olitzky and Rabbi Daniel Judson

MELANIE HALL / *IN OUR IMAGE*

God is like the Unconscious of the universe, only occasionally visible but always at work.

—Rabbi Lawrence Kushner, *The Book of Words:
Talking Spiritual Life, Living Spiritual Talk*

My First Four Months

These are the things I've learned to do so far: _____

_____

_____

_____

_____

Fill in Dates and Descriptions of "Firsts"

My daily routine is: _____

_____

_____

_____

_____

place photos here

Light shine upon us
Our people have increased
And our joy is made great
For we have borne a child
May there be no end of peace

—from Isaiah 9

These are some of the things that make me happy: _____

_____

These are some of the times that I'm cranky: _____

_____

_____

My parents had these thoughts about what I've done and how I've changed
since I was born:

_____

_____

_____

_____

_____

_____

_____

God of our mothers, Sarah, Rivkah, Rachel, and Leah, You remembered me
when I longed for this child and in the pain of labor, and You have brought
me, rejoicing, to hold this infant in my arms. Now I turn to You again,
hoping to feed this child as You feed all living creatures, out of Your boundless lovingkindness; and I trust in You, that in Your goodness You surely will
not let my child lack sustenance, neither now nor ever, for the sake of Your
great Name. Let any pain that I may feel as I nurse this child be submerged
in my joy as I watch the miracle of my flourishing baby; and keep us from
any misfortune that may cause suffering to my child or to me between now
and the time that my child is safely weaned. May Your goodness teach me
to help my child grow both now in my arms and in all the years You grant us
together. For You are the God who has always given me good things.
Blessed are You, God, who sustains all.

—Elisheva S. Urbas

Months 5–8

These days I'm doing a lot of things for the first time: _____

_____

_____

_____

_____

_____

_____

Fill in Dates and Descriptions of "Firsts"

I like to spend my days: _____

_____

_____

_____

place photos here

God sends us children to teach us what God has given up
trying to teach us in every other way.

—Rabbi Lawrence Kushner, *Invisible Lines of Connection:*
Sacred Stories of the Ordinary

Blessed are you who bear the divine presence.

—from *The New Jewish Baby Book: Names, Ceremonies and Customs—*
A Guide for Today's Families, by Anita Diamant

These are some of my favorite things: _____

_____

_____

These are some of the things I don't like: _____

_____

My parents had these thoughts about all of my accomplishments:

_____

_____

_____

_____

_____

_____

_____

_____

Our mothers had blessings for occasions that we may not think of as a time for blessings. For example, many said a blessing when a child's first tooth emerged: "Your wonders and care over all creatures are so great and numerous they cannot be recounted. When a child begins to wean, You give him [or her] teeth with which to chew. For the precious gift, the little pearl I have found in my child's mouth, I thank You, and praise your Name."

—Rabbi Nina Beth Cardin, "Blessings throughout the Day,"
from *The Rituals & Practices of a Jewish Life:
A Handbook for Personal Spiritual Renewal*,
edited by Rabbi Kerry M. Olitzky and Rabbi Daniel Judson

MELANIE HALL / IN OUR IMAGE

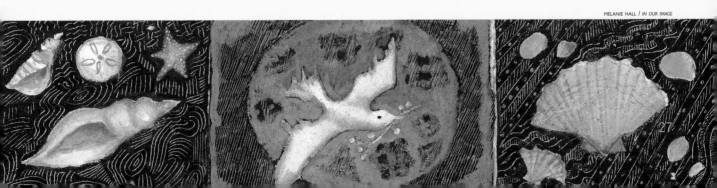

Months 9–12

I'm doing new things all the time now, like: _____

_____

_____

_____

_____

_____

_____

Fill in Dates and Descriptions of "Firsts"

During the day, I: _____

_____

_____

_____

_____

place photos here

By the breath of children God sustains the world.

Shabbat 119b

May your heart be filled with intuition and your words be
filled with insight.

Talmud

The best toys I have are: _____

_____

_____

My favorite music is: _____

_____

_____

When my parents see how quickly I'm growing, they think and feel:

_____

_____

_____

_____

_____

_____

_____

_____

Just as my child has arrived safely into the world and into my life, may my child be blessed with abundant love, guidance, and protection.

Enable me to be fully present for this new and wondrous life.

Help me to be a wise and loving parent. Help me to be patient and kind, to be a teacher and worthy model. And when I need support, may the community provide a home and haven for this child through the years.

—from *The Book of Jewish Sacred Practices: CLAL's Guide to Everyday & Holiday Rituals & Blessings,* edited by Rabbi Irwin Kula and Vanessa L. Ochs, Ph.D.

My First Birthday

Yom Huledet Sameach! Happy Birthday!

Family and friends came to celebrate my first birthday with me.
Here is a picture of the party:

place photo here

People gave me presents—toys, clothes, and lots of Jewish books and music.
Here's a list of who gave me what:

_____

_____

_____

_____

_____

_____

On my first birthday, my grandparents or other relatives had these blessings for me:

_____

_____

_____

Ad me'ah v'esrim!

עַד מֵאָה וְעֶשְׂרִים.

May you live until one hundred and twenty!

> Hear, O my child, and receive my sayings; and the years of
> thy life shall be many.

Proverbs 4:1

*There is a modern Jewish tradition of making prayers or poems
out of the first letters of a child's name, based on the ancient Jewish tradition of piyyut,
poems—often written as acrostics—for the prayer service.*

In honor of my first birthday, my parents found meaningful lines in Jewish texts
and came up with this acrostic using my Hebrew name:

Letter

_____ _____

_____ _____

_____ _____

_____ _____

_____ _____

_____ _____

_____ _____

_____ _____

_____ _____

_____ _____

_____ _____

LAWRENCE KUSHNER / *THE BOOK OF LETTERS*

The OTIYOT [Hebrew letters]
are more than just the signs for sounds.
They are symbols whose shape and
name, placement in the alphabet,
and words they begin put them each
at the center of a unique
spiritual constellation.
They are themselves holy.
They are vessels carrying within the
light of the Boundless One.

—Rabbi Lawrence Kushner,
*The Book of Letters:
A Mystical Alef-bait*

At One Year...

I'm doing: _____

_____

_____

_____

I'm saying: _____

_____

_____

I'm eating: _____

_____

_____

My friends are: _____

_____

_____

My favorite foods, toys, books, songs, people, and other things are: _____

_____

_____

_____

Things I don't like: _____

_____

_____

Adonai is mindful of us, will bless the house of Israel; will
bless the house of Aaron; will bless those who revere
Adonai, the little ones and the big ones together.

Psalms 115:12–13

PHOEBE STONE / IN GOD'S NAME

Songs and rhymes my parents made up, and when we use them:

_____

_____

_____

_____

Our mealtime rituals: _____

_____

_____

_____

Bathtime rituals: _____

_____

_____

_____

Bedtime rituals: _____

_____

_____

_____

Ritual creates its own feedback. We hold hands with a child as the sun rises, and we sense, in a way we never did before, that the world is being reborn before our eyes. Suddenly we are in the presence of the unutterable. Believing now in the world's rebirth, we choose to make that handholding part of our daily lives, perhaps adding some word of prayer, perhaps creating a miniritual. Along with our child, we find language to express what cannot be spoken. Using that language over and over, we are confirmed in our initial hunch. The world is pregnant with meaning and the sunrise with the day.

PHOEBE STONE / IN GOD'S NAME

—Rabbi Nancy Fuchs-Kreimer, *Parenting As a Spiritual Journey: Deepening Ordinary & Extraordinary Events into Sacred Occasions*

At Two Years....

This is how I spend my days: _____

_____

_____

_____

These are some of my relatives, and they want to tell me: _____

_____

_____

_____

These are my special babysitters/nannies and what they have to say about me:

_____

_____

_____

These are my neighbors and people I know from my community and what they have to say about me: _____

_____

_____

_____

All life is within community and each of us is inextricably connected to those around us…. Within community, we hope to be nourished and sustained so we can create, reach our goals, and be transformed. Within community, we may experience the "whole" becoming greater than the sum of the parts. The power of community has been an essential theme in the story of the Jewish people.

PHOEBE STONE / IN GOD'S NAME

—Rabbi James L. Mirel and Karen Bonnell Werth,
Stepping Stones to Jewish Spiritual Living:
Walking the Path, Morning, Noon, and Night

As a baby grows into childhood, the occasions for blessings are nearly limitless. Below is a list of special blessings that will come in handy for a child just beginning to notice the wonders of the world:

For firsts, celebrating the first time in the cycle of a year, or in one's life, that a special event occurs—

Barukh ata Adonay Eloheynu melekh ha'olam she'hecheyanu v'kiy'manu v'higiyanu la'zman ha'zeh.

בָּרוּךְ אַתָּה, יְיָ אֱלֹהֵינוּ, מֶלֶךְ הָעוֹלָם, שֶׁהֶחֱיָנוּ וְקִיְּמָנוּ וְהִגִּיעָנוּ לַזְּמַן הַזֶּה.

Blessed are You who has kept us in life, sustained us, and enabled us to reach this season.

For beauty in the natural world (people, animals, trees, fields)—

Barukh ata Adonay Eloheynu melekh ha'olam sheh'kakhah lo ba'olamo.

בָּרוּךְ אַתָּה, יְיָ אֱלֹהֵינוּ, מֶלֶךְ הָעוֹלָם, שֶׁכָּכָה לוֹ בָּעוֹלָמוֹ.

Blessed are You who has such as this in the universe.

For lightening, or natural wonders like a comet, majestic mountains, great rivers—

Barukh ata Adonay Eloheynu melekh ha'olam oseh ma'asey v'reishit.

בָּרוּךְ אַתָּה, יְיָ אֱלֹהֵינוּ, מֶלֶךְ הָעוֹלָם, עֹשֶׂה מַעֲשֵׂה בְרֵאשִׁית.

Blessed are You who does the work of Creation.

For seeing a rainbow in the sky—

Barukh ata Adonay Eloheynu melekh ha'olam zokheyr ha'brit, v'neh'ehman biv'rito, v'kayam b'maamaro.

בָּרוּךְ אַתָּה, יְיָ אֱלֹהֵינוּ, מֶלֶךְ הָעוֹלָם, זוֹכֵר הַבְּרִית, וְנֶאֱמָן בִּבְרִיתוֹ, וְקַיָּם בְּמַאֲמָרוֹ.

Blessed are You who remembers and is faithful to the covenant.

Upon hearing thunder—

Barukh ata Adonay Eloheynu melekh ha'olam sheh'kocho u'gevurato maley olam.

בָּרוּךְ אַתָּה, יְיָ אֱלֹהֵינוּ, מֶלֶךְ הָעוֹלָם, שֶׁכֹּחוֹ וּגְבוּרָתוֹ מָלֵא עוֹלָם.

Blessed are You whose strength and power fill the universe.

—Blessings from *The Path of Blessing: Experiencing the Energy and Abundance of the Divine,* by Marcia Prager

MELANIE HALL / IN OUR IMAGE

At Three Years...

My favorite Jewish/Hebrew books are: _____

_____

_____

My favorite Jewish/Hebrew songs are: _____

_____

_____

When I'm playing outdoors, I like to: _____

_____

_____

And these are the games I like to play indoors: _____

_____

_____

May you flourish as you become who you are meant to be.

—from *The Book of Jewish Sacred Practices: CLAL's Guide to Everyday & Holiday Rituals & Blessings,* edited by Rabbi Irwin Kula and Vanessa L. Ochs, Ph.D.

We must learn the dance because life at its best is the seamless integration of all aspects of self: worlds seen and worlds experienced, the world of doing and the world of being.

We must dance between our physical needs and spiritual needs because the human experience demands that we eat and that we be nourished.

—Rabbi Karyn D. Kedar, *The Dance of the Dolphin: Finding Prayer, Perspective and Meaning in the Stories of Our Lives*

PHOEBE STONE / *IN GOD'S NAME*

BACKGROUND: AVI KATZ / *THE JEWISH FAMILY FUN BOOK*

The First Haircut!

Some traditional Jews do not cut their child's hair until the child is three years of age. This custom reflects the Torah passage that says you should not pick the fruit from a tree until it is three years old. This can be a big celebration with family and friends (all of whom help with the haircut)!

I got my first haircut on: _____ at _____.

Date   *Location*

Here's a picture of me before my first haircut:

place photo here

And after my first haircut:

place photo here

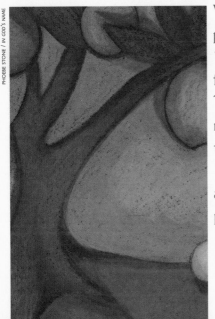

PHOEBE STONE / *IN GOD'S NAME*

While walking along a road, a sage saw a man planting a carob tree. He asked him, "How long will it take for this tree to bear fruit?" "Seventy years," replied the man. The sage then asked, "Are you so healthy a man that you expect to live that length of time and eat its fruit?" The man answered, "I found a fruitful world, because my ancestors planted it for me. Likewise I am planting for my children."

Talmud *Ta'anit* 23a

We dedicate our child to Torah,
To a never-ending fascination with study and learning
With a book, he/she will never be alone.

We dedicate our child to *chupah*,
To never-ending growth as a human being capable of
   giving and receiving love.
With a loving mate, he/she will never be alone.

We dedicate our child to *ma'asim tovim*,
To a never-ending concern for family and community,
   justice and charity.
If he/she cares for others, he/she will never be alone.

We pray for wisdom to help our child achieve
   these things,
To fulfill the needs of his/her mind and body,
To be strong when he/she needs us to be strong,
To be gentle when he/she needs us to be gentle,
But always there when he/she needs us.
The birth of a child is a miracle of renewal.
We stand together this day, contemplating a miracle.

—from *The New Jewish Baby Book: Names, Ceremonies and Customs—
A Guide for Today's Families,* by Anita Diamant

Jewish Holy Days & Holidays

Do you want to know the joy of celebration?
Dance with a Torah scroll on Simchat Torah. Do you want to know the power of a community that values freedom as our highest aspiration? Sit at a Passover seder year after year, remembering that "we were slaves to Pharaoh in Egypt." No matter how old you are, you can keep the child inside you from disappearing, just by showing up at Purim to read the Book of Esther and enjoy the fun that accompanies it. I know what it is to give thanks because I celebrate Sukkot, and I know the joy of learning because I have a holiday of revelation called Shavuot…. Hanukkah finds me zealous for the freedom for others that my ancestors once attained for me, and the High Holidays never fail to thrill me with feeling that I have been reborn along with the new year, permitted to hope for goodness and happiness in my life and in the lives of those I love.

—Rabbi Lawrence A. Hoffman, *The Way Into Jewish Prayer*

Shabbat

The root of the word *Shabbat* means to "cease" or "desist." To observe Shabbat means to cease our work life and break our daily routine every seventh day, making that day holy. Shabbat is to be a day of enjoying God's world rather than doing battle with it; a day of relaxation rather than struggle, a time to live in harmony rather than to achieve domination.

—Rabbi Arthur Green, *These Are the Words: A Vocabulary of Jewish Spiritual Life*

My favorite thing about Shabbat is: _____

_____

_____

Family Blessings, Celebrating with Guests, the Candles, Challah, Singing

I helped light the candles for the first time: _____

_____

Date, Age, Reaction

I began to learn the blessings for the candles, wine, and challah: _____

_____

Date, Age, Reaction

I went to my first "Tot Shabbat" with other children: _____

_____

Date, Age, Place, Reaction

By observing Shabbat we become God's collaborators in Creation. When we rest on the seventh day and give rest to the world around us, just as God did on that first Shabbat, we increase the tranquility and harmony in the universe. Being mindful of the day and relating to it through concrete actions grounded in mitzvah, we infuse our personal universes with holiness and wholeness.

—Moshe Mykoff, *7th Heaven:*
Celebrating Shabbat with Rebbe Nachman of Breslov

Blessing for Daughters

Yesimekh Elohim ke'Sarah Rivka Rahel ve'Leah

יְשִׂימֵךְ אֱלֹהִים כְּשָׂרָה רִבְקָה רָחֵל וְלֵאָה.

(May) God make you like Sarah,
Rebecca, Rachel, and Leah.

place photo here

Blessing for Sons

Y'simkha Elohim k'Efrayim vekiMenashe

יְשִׂימְךָ אֱלֹהִים כְּאֶפְרַיִם וְכִמְנַשֶּׁה.

(May) God make you like Ephraim and Menasseh.

This is how we make Shabbat in our home:

_____

_____

_____

These are some of the things we do on Saturdays to honor Shabbat:

_____

_____

Other reflections and remembrances of our family's Shabbat celebrations:

_____

_____

_____

The real world of Shabbat is made up of tablecloths stained with repeated use, family jokes that are so well known that just a look triggers a laugh, hugs, and the feel and the taste of warm challah. It is this real-world Shabbat that bonds couples closer together, that creates significant family moments, that roots Jewish identity.

—Dr. Ron Wolfson, *Shabbat: The Family Guide to Preparing for and Celebrating the Sabbath*

Rosh Hashanah & Yom Kippur

L'shana Tova! Happy New Year!

Rosh Hashanah, literally the "head of the year," is also the Day of Judgment, the Day of Remembrance. Though not formally named as such, it is also the day of rebirth, the time of renewal.... Yom Kippur is the holiest and most awesome day on the Hebrew calendar. It is called a "Sabbath of Sabbaths"; all work that is forbidden on the Sabbath is forbidden on Yom Kippur as well.... Yom Kippur is also one of the most ancient Jewish festivals.

—Rabbi Arthur Green, *These Are the Words: A Vocabulary of Jewish Spiritual Life*

I went to synagogue to hear the blowing of the shofar (ram's horn) for the first time:

_____

_____

_____

Date, Name of Synagogue, Reaction to the Sound of the Shofar

I first tasted apples and challah dipped in honey: _____

_____

Date, Place, Reaction

The first time I joined my community for *tashlich* (symbolically throwing bread crumbs into moving water to "cast our sins into the sea"): _____

_____

_____

Date, Place, Reaction

Today is the birthday of the world.

Rosh Hashanah liturgy

AVI KATZ / THE JEWISH FAMILY FUN BOOK

May each sound of the shofar awaken me to the sacred presence in all things.

—from *The Book of Jewish Sacred Practices: CLAL's Guide to Everyday & Holiday Rituals & Blessings*, edited by Rabbi Irwin Kula and Vanessa L. Ochs, Ph.D.

How we celebrate Rosh Hashanah as a family:

_____

_____

_____

Our family Rosh Hashanah resolutions:

_____

_____

Other Rosh Hashanah and Yom Kippur reflections and remembrances:

_____

_____

_____

_____

Happy New Year! Rosh Hashanah … marks the beginning of the Jewish year. It's a time of joy and celebration—of blowing the shofar to alert everyone to this important holiday—and of eating sweets like apples and honey in hopes of a sweet year. It's also a great chance to spend quality time with your family … to reflect together and make new year's resolutions.

—Danielle Dardashti and Roni Sarig, *The Jewish Family Fun Book: Holiday Projects, Everyday Activities, and Travel Ideas with Jewish Themes*

AVI KATZ / *THE JEWISH FAMILY FUN BOOK*

Sukkot

Sukkot, the festival of the fall full moon … is a harvest festival, "the season of ingathering." As we gather the produce of the field into our homes for the winter, so does God gather us into God's special place, the *sukkah*.

—Rabbi Arthur Green, *These Are the Words: A Vocabulary of Jewish Spiritual Life*

I first ate in a *sukkah*: _____

_____

_____

_____

Date, Location, Reactions

I helped decorate a *sukkah:* _____

_____

_____

Date, Location, Decorations

I shook the *lulav* (palm branches) and held the *etrog* (citron): _____

_____

_____

Date, Reactions

Just as we have found beauty together as we have dwelled in this *sukkah*, may we find beauty together all year as we dwell in each other's lives.

—from *The Book of Jewish Sacred Practices: CLAL's Guide to Everyday & Holiday Rituals & Blessings*, edited by Rabbi Irwin Kula and Vanessa L. Ochs, Ph.D.

"Thank you, God,…I love the *sukkah!*"
"Thank you, God,…for giving us the strength to put up the *sukkah* without its falling down…"
"…for making each of us different and special like the *lulav* and *etrog*…"
"…and for allowing us to live together with those differences in a *sukkat shalom* … a *sukkah* of peace."

—Rahel Musleah and Rabbi Michael Klayman, *Sharing Blessings: Children's Stories for Exploring the Spirit of the Jewish Holidays*

BACKGROUND: AVI KATZ / THE JEWISH FAMILY FUN BOOK

place photos here

Sukkot is called "the season of our joy," and is meant to be the most joyous of all the festivals. This is not the frolicking joy of Purim, but a happiness born of deep satiety at the harvest and gratitude for God's gifts.

—Rabbi Arthur Green, *These Are the Words: A Vocabulary of Jewish Spiritual Life*

How we celebrate Sukkot as a family:

_____
_____
_____

Some of the things for which we are thankful:

_____
_____

Other reflections and remembrances about Sukkot:

_____
_____
_____
_____

The holiday of Sukkot … is one of the most active holidays around—an excellent chance for shared family experiences. Best of all, it's the time to build a *sukkah*, a homemade Jewish hut where families eat and even sleep … for the seven days of this holiday.

—Danielle Dardashti and Roni Sarig, *The Jewish Family Fun Book: Holiday Projects, Everyday Activities, and Travel Ideas with Jewish Themes*

Simchat Torah

Simchat Torah (literally: "the joy of Torah") is the concluding day of the fall festival cycle....
On this day, the annual cycle of Torah reading is concluded and begins again, showing the
constancy of Torah and its place in the life of the Jewish people.

—Rabbi Arthur Green, *These Are the Words: A Vocabulary of Jewish Spiritual Life*

My first Simchat Torah: _____

_____

_____

Date, Place, Reactions

The first Simchat Torah I participated in by dancing, waving a flag, or marching:

_____

_____

_____

Date, Place, Reactions

While the adults are the ones who read from the Torah,
Simchat Torah is also a children's holiday. At synagogue,
there's singing and dancing for all ages, and candy is given
out. Plus, this is the only holiday when kids come up to the
Torah to make a blessing (an *aliyah*), an honor usually
reserved for people older than bar and bat mitzvah age....
Simchat Torah is a rare opportunity when having a
party during services is not only acceptable, it's entirely
appropriate!

—Danielle Dardashti and Roni Sarig, *The Jewish Family Fun Book:
Holiday Projects, Everyday Activities, and Travel Ideas with Jewish Themes*

AVI KATZ / THE JEWISH FAMILY FUN BOOK

place photos here

This is how we celebrate Simchat Torah as a family:

_____
_____
_____

These are the friends we dance with on Simchat Torah:

_____
_____

Other reflections and remembrances about our family's Simchat Torah:

_____
_____
_____
_____

Dancing with the Torah is like dancing with your newborn children and your parents at the same time. We dress the Torah like a newborn and cradle it, kiss it, protect it. We respect the Torah like a parent, challenge it, and learn from its words.

—from *The Book of Jewish Sacred Practices: CLAL's Guide to Everyday & Holiday Rituals & Blessings,* edited by Rabbi Irwin Kula and Vanessa L. Ochs, Ph.D.

Hanukkah

Hanukkah (literally: "dedication") ... celebrates the victory of the Macabbean rebels over the Hellenistic rulers in the year 165 B.C.E.... The Macabbean revolt was a Jewish reaction to ... the threatened disappearance of the distinctive religious culture of the Jews.

—Rabbi Arthur Green, *These Are the Words: A Vocabulary of Jewish Spiritual Life*

The first time I helped light the candles and sing the blessings: _____

_____

_____

_____

Date, Place, Reactions

The first time I spun a dreidel: _____

_____

Date, Place, Reactions

My first taste of foods fried in oil like latkes (potato pancakes) or *soofganiyot* (jelly doughnuts): _____

_____

Date, Place, Reactions

The first time I unwrapped my own presents: _____

_____

_____

_____

Date, Place, Reactions

The first time I gave presents: _____

_____

_____

_____

Date, Gifts, to Whom They Were Given

The ritual of lighting the *hanukkiyah* is an act of publicizing one's Jewish belief in the miracles which God can work in the constant availability of hope. As each generation passes this ancient custom on, parents are constantly teaching their children that the battle can be won, that darkness can be overcome, that—inspired and enlightened by God's teachings—almost anything is possible.

—Dr. Ron Wolfson, *Hanukkah: The Family Guide to Spiritual Celebration*

BRIDGETT TAYLOR

This is how we celebrate Hanukkah as a family:

_____

_____

_____

These are some of the important lessons of Hanukkah:

_____

_____

Other Hanukkah reflections and remembrances:

_____

_____

_____

My home is the place where I celebrate life, mark the seasons, welcome guests, light candles, remember the past, dream about the future, and open my heart to the present. At Hanukkah, may I rededicate my home to the values and relationships I hold sacred…. May these Hanukkah lights guide us to appreciate people and things for what they are.

—from *The Book of Jewish Sacred Practices: CLAL's Guide to Everyday & Holiday Rituals & Blessings,* edited by Rabbi Irwin Kula and Vanessa L. Ochs, Ph.D.

Tu B'Shvat

Tu B'Shvat comes in January or February. It is best known as the festival of trees and is a time when people plant trees in Israel. Mystically, it is a time when the will to live first finds expression, when the sap that will produce blossoms in the springtime begins to flow.

—Rabbi David A. Cooper, *The Handbook of Jewish Meditation Practices: A Guide for Enriching the Sabbath and Other Days of Your Life*

A tree was planted in Israel in my name: _____

_____

Date and Name of Person(s) Who Had the Tree Planted

I planted something for the first time: _____

_____

_____

Date, Place, What Was Planted, Reaction

I saw what I planted begin to sprout: _____

_____

_____

Date and Reaction

My favorite fruits are: _____

_____

_____

On Tu B'Shvat, many Jews direct their attention toward the produce in the Land of Israel and reflect on the way they treat nature.... We can invite people over to celebrate with us, eat fruits associated with Israel, have a Tu B'Shvat seder, and maybe even plant a tree that will endure for many years to come.

—Danielle Dardashti and Roni Sarig, *The Jewish Family Fun Book: Holiday Projects, Everyday Activities, and Travel Ideas with Jewish Themes*

place photos here

This is how we celebrate Tu B'Shvat as a family:

_____

_____

_____

As a family, we are helping to protect the environment by:

_____

_____

Other reflections and remembrances about our family's Tu B'Shvat:

_____

_____

_____

_____

We can watch for crocuses when they poke up from the ground in the spring. We can play in the leaves when they turn gold and red and brown in the fall. During the summer, we can listen to birds sing. Even now ... we can watch squirrels scampering up the trees.

—Rahel Musleah and Rabbi Michael Klayman,
*Sharing Blessings: Children's Stories for
Exploring the Spirit of the Jewish Holidays*

PHOEBE STONE / IN GOD'S NAME

51

Purim

The festival of Purim ... commemorates the events of the biblical Book of Esther *(megillah)*, the defeat of wicked Haman and the foiling of his plot to kill the Jews throughout the Persian Empire.... Hasidic teaching sees Purim as a time of hidden miracles. The story of Esther, which appears as a mostly secular tale in the Bible, is used to show that the Divine Hand is present even in the events that seem ordinary.

—Rabbi Arthur Green, *These Are the Words: A Vocabulary of Jewish Spiritual Life*

The first time I went to synagogue to hear the reading of *Megillat Esther:*

_____

_____

Date, Place, Reactions

My first taste of *hamantaschen* (traditional Purim pastry shaped like Haman's hat):

_____

Date, Flavor, Reactions

My first Purim costume:

_____

Date, Character, Reactions

The first time I used a *grogger* (noisemaker):

_____

Date, Reactions

The first time I gave *mishloach manot* (a basket of cakes, sweets, and fruits) to a friend, relative, or person in need:

_____

_____

Date, Contents, Recipient, Reactions

> Laughter is so important that Jews have institutionalized it into a holiday. Purim does more than celebrate the foiled attempts of anti-Semites everywhere; it makes us laugh at ourselves.
>
> —Rabbi Lawrence Kushner, *The Book of Words: Talking Spiritual Life, Living Spiritual Talk*

place photos here

This is how we celebrate Purim as a family:

_____

_____

_____

Giving to others is a big part of Purim. Here are some of the ways we contribute *tzedakah* throughout the year:

_____

_____

Other reflections and remembrances about our family's Purim:

_____

_____

_____

There are four *mitsvot* associated with the celebration of Purim…. These are the reading of the *megillah*, the exchanging of gifts (usually cakes and sweets), giving to the poor, and merry feasting.
—Rabbi Arthur Green, *These Are the Words: A Vocabulary of Jewish Spiritual Life*

La'yehudim hayetah orah vesimchah vesason v'ikar.
לַיְּהוּדִים הָיְתָה אוֹרָה וְשִׂמְחָה וְשָׂשֹׂן וִיקָר.
There was light, joy, gladness and honor for the Jewish people.
—Rahel Musleah and Rabbi Michael Klayman, *Sharing Blessings: Children's Stories for Exploring the Spirit of the Jewish Holidays*

Pesah

Pesah is the festival of spring, liberation, and renewal. Since biblical times, Pesah has commemorated Israel's Exodus from Egypt, which is the paradigm for movements of national liberation as well as the great example for spiritual and personal liberation wherever the Bible is read and taught.

—Rabbi Arthur Green, *These Are the Words: A Vocabulary of Jewish Spiritual Life*

I went to my first seder: _____

_____

_____

Date, Place, Reactions

I tasted matzah for the first time: _____

_____

Date, Place, Reactions

I looked for the *afikomen* (piece of matzah hidden during the seder) for the first time:

_____

_____

_____

Date, Place, Reactions

I began to learn the Four Questions and Passover songs: _____

_____

_____

_____

Date, Place, Reactions

Bekhol-dor vador chayav adam lirot et atsmo ke'ilu hu yatsa mimitsrayim.

בְּכָל־דּוֹר וָדוֹר חַיָּב אָדָם לִרְאוֹת אֶת עַצְמוֹ כְּאִלּוּ הוּא יָצָא מִמִּצְרָיִם.

In every generation we should picture ourselves leaving Egypt and standing at Sinai.

—Rahel Musleah and Rabbi Michael Klayman, *Sharing Blessings: Children's Stories for Exploring the Spirit of the Jewish Holidays*

place photos here

This is how we celebrate Pesah as a family:

_____

_____

_____

These are some of the things we do to make our family seder special:

_____

_____

_____

Other reflections and remembrances about our family's Pesah:

_____

_____

_____

Seder nights are magic. They both transcend and unite history. Torah teaches us that the first Seder took place on the eve of the Exodus…. For generations, we have sat together to remember, retell, recreate, and relive that Exodus experience. Over time, the Seder has become more than an historic remembrance; it has evolved its own memories and significance. We cannot return to the lessons of that first Seder night in Egypt without its being enriched by the memories of our own Seder celebrations.

—Dr. Ron Wolfson, *Passover: The Family Guide to Spiritual Celebration*

Shavuot

The Torah's fullest description of Shavuot (Deuteronomy 16:9–12) sees it as a joyous time celebrating the full growth of the crops.... Only in post-biblical writings does Shavuot come to be known as the day the Torah was given.... The Kabbalists originated a custom, now very widespread, of staying awake all night on Shavuot eve and studying Torah as preparation for receiving Torah once again at dawn....The covenant at Sinai is often depicted as the symbolic marriage of God and the Jewish people. In Sephardic synagogues, a special *ketubah* or marriage contract is read in the synagogue to celebrate that occasion.

—Rabbi Arthur Green, *These Are the Words: A Vocabulary of Jewish Spiritual Life*

I first ate cheese or berry blintzes (thin, rolled pancakes eaten on Shavuot to celebrate the harvest): _____

_____

Date, Place, Reaction

I picked flowers for the first time: _____

_____

Date, Place, Reaction

I began to learn the Ten Commandments: _____

_____

_____

Date, Place, Reaction

Barukh ata Adonay Eloheynu melekh ha'olam asher kideshanu bemitsvotav vetsivanu la'asok bedivrei torah.

בָּרוּךְ אַתָּה, יְיָ אֱלֹהֵינוּ, מֶלֶךְ הָעוֹלָם,
אֲשֶׁר קִדְּשָׁנוּ בְּמִצְוֹתָיו וְצִוָּנוּ לַעֲסוֹק בְּדִבְרֵי תוֹרָה.

Praised are You, Adonai our God,
whose Torah guides us wherever we go,
whatever we do, for a good and Jewish life.

—Rahel Musleah and Rabbi Michael Klayman,
*Sharing Blessings: Children's Stories for
Exploring the Spirit of the Jewish Holidays*

place photos here

This is how we celebrate Shavuot as a family:

_____

_____

_____

These are some of the values most important to our family:

_____

_____

_____

_____

Other reflections and remembrances about our family's Shavuot:

_____

_____

_____

For on Shavuot, we celebrate the moment when we stood at Sinai and became a people. Just as the Passover seder allows us to experience the movement from slavery to freedom, studying together with Jews from diverse communities on the eve of Shavuot allows us to reenact the time we all stood at Sinai. In sacred conversation, we challenge each other to see our ancient text anew. We celebrate our unity by asking the questions we can't answer alone.

—from *The Book of Jewish Sacred Practices: CLAL's Guide to Everyday & Holiday Rituals & Blessings*, edited by Rabbi Irwin Kula and Vanessa L. Ochs, Ph.D.

Our God and God of our fathers and mothers, raise this child to a long life, a life of peace and well-being, a life of blessing and sustenance, a life of health, a life of devotion and fear of transgression, a life without shame or disgrace, a life of riches and honor, a life shaped by our love of Torah and devotion to God, a life in which the requests of our heart be fulfilled for the good. Amen.

—Debra Nussbaum Cohen, *Celebrating Your New Jewish Daughter: Creating Jewish Ways to Welcome Baby Girls into the Covenant*

Everything in God's creation has its distinctive melody, a rhythm and life-beat that it alone plays. This is especially true of humanity. Each of us has the song we sing in this world, an evolving ballad that is uniquely his or her own.

—Moshe Mykoff, *7th Heaven: Celebrating Shabbat with Rebbe Nachman of Breslov*

JOANI KELLER ROTHENBERG / CAIN AND ABEL

Important Information About Me

BETHANNE ANDERSEN / NOAH'S WIFE

Caring for the bodies of children is an opportunity to reflect on their beauty, on their quality as images of the Divine. The Bible forbids making pictures or statues of God because every human being is God's image. Caring for the image of God is a commandment.

—Rabbi Nancy Fuchs-Kreimer, *Parenting As a Spiritual Journey: Deepening Ordinary & Extraordinary Events into Sacred Occasions*

My Social Security Number is: _____

My pediatrician's name is: _____

I had this immunization: On this date:

_____

_____

_____

_____

_____

_____

_____

_____

This is the order and dates my teeth came in:

_____

_____

_____

_____

_____

Other health information:

_____

_____

_____

_____

Barukh ata Adonay Eloheynu melekh ha'olam,
yotzer ha'adam.

בָּרוּךְ אַתָּה, יְיָ אֱלֹהֵינוּ, מֶלֶךְ הָעוֹלָם, יוֹצֵר הָאָדָם.

Praised are You, Adonai our God,
Source of the Universe, Creator of humanity.

PHOEBE STONE / IN GOD'S NAME

How I've Grown!

Date	Age	Height	Weight	Notes

The goal of spirituality is the bringing together of seeing, hearing, and doing into one whole person. It is to see yourself mirrored in the heavens above and to realize that the Holy One created you personally to help complete the work of repairing the world.

—Rabbi Lawrence Kushner, *The Book of Miracles:
A Young Person's Guide to Jewish Spiritual Awareness*

Some Jewish Lights Books for the Family

Because Nothing Looks Like God, Rabbi Lawrence and Karen Kushner (Ages 4 and up; illus. by Dawn W. Majewski) What is God like? This wondrous book shows children how God is with us every day, in every way.

But God Remembered: Stories of Women from Creation to the Promised Land, Rabbi Sandy Eisenberg Sasso (Ages 8 and up; illus. by Bethanne Andersen)

Cain & Abel: Finding the Fruits of Peace, Rabbi Sandy Eisenberg Sasso (Ages 5 and up; illus. by Joani Keller Rothenberg) A spiritual conversation-starter about anger and how to deal with it—for children and grown-ups to share.

Celebrating Your New Jewish Daughter: Creating Jewish Ways to Welcome Baby Girls into the Covenant, Debra Nussbaum Cohen

God's Paintbrush, Rabbi Sandy Eisenberg Sasso (Ages 4 and up; illus. by Annette Compton) Invites children of all faiths and backgrounds to encounter God through moments in their own lives.

Hanukkah: The Family Guide to Spiritual Celebration, Dr. Ron Wolfson

How Does God Make Things Happen? Rabbi Lawrence and Karen Kushner (Ages 0–4; board book, illus. by Dawn W. Majewski) Abridged from *Because Nothing Looks Like God*, specially adapted to delight and inspire younger readers. A SkyLight Paths book.

In God's Name, Rabbi Sandy Eisenberg Sasso (Ages 4 and up; illus. by Phoebe Stone) A modern fable about the search for God's name, celebrating the diversity and ultimate harmony of people of all faiths.

In Our Image: God's First Creatures, Nancy Sohn Swartz (Ages 4 and up; illus. by Melanie Hall) In a playful twist to the Genesis story, God asks all of nature to offer gifts to humankind—with a promise that the humans would care for creation in return.

The Jewish Family Fun Book: Holiday Projects, Everyday Activities, and Travel Ideas with Jewish Themes, Danielle Dardashti and Roni Sarig; illustrated by Avi Katz

Naamah, Noah's Wife, Rabbi Sandy Eisenberg Sasso (Ages 0–4; board book, illus. by Bethanne Andersen) Abridged from *Noah's Wife: The Story of Naamah*, specially adapted to delight and inspire younger readers. A SkyLight Paths book.

The New Jewish Baby Book: Names, Ceremonies and Customs—A Guide for Today's Families, Anita Diamant

Noah's Wife: The Story of Naamah, Rabbi Sandy Eisenberg Sasso (Ages 4 and up; illus. by Bethanne Andersen) When God tells Noah to bring the animals of the world onto the ark, God also calls on Naamah, Noah's wife, to save each plant on Earth.

Parenting As a Spiritual Journey: Deepening Ordinary & Extraordinary Events into Sacred Occasions, Rabbi Nancy Fuchs-Kreimer

Shabbat: The Family Guide to Preparing for and Celebrating the Sabbath, Dr. Ron Wolfson

Sharing Blessings: Children's Stories for Exploring the Spirit of the Jewish Holidays, Rahel Musleah and Rabbi Michael Klayman (Ages 6 and up; illus. by Mary O'Keefe Young)

What Is God's Name, Rabbi Sandy Eisenberg Sasso (Ages 0–4; board book; illus. by Phoebe Stone) Abridged from *In God's Name*, specially adapted to delight and inspire younger readers. A SkyLight Paths book.

For more information about these and other Jewish Lights books, call 1-800-962-4544 or visit www.jewishlights.com

About the Contributors

Anita Diamant is a prize-winning journalist and the author of *The New Jewish Baby Book: Names, Ceremomies & Customs— A Guide for Today's Families* and the novel *The Red Tent*.

Sandy Eisenberg Sasso is rabbi of Congregation Beth-El Zedeck in Indianapolis. She is active in the interfaith community and has written and lectured on the renewal of spirituality and the discovery of religious imagination in children of all faiths. She is the second woman ever to be ordained a rabbi and the first rabbi to become a mother. Her award-winning books include *God Said Amen, God's Paintbrush, In God's Name, But God Remembered: Stories of Women from Creation to the Promised Land, God in Between,* and *Cain & Abel: Finding the Fruits of Peace.*

About Jewish Lights

People of all faiths and backgrounds yearn for books that attract, engage, educate, and spiritually inspire.

Our principal goal is to stimulate thought and help all people learn about who the Jewish People are, where they come from, and what the future can be made to hold. While people of our diverse Jewish heritage are the primary audience, our books speak to people in the Christian world as well and will broaden their understanding of Judaism and the roots of their own faith.

We bring to you authors who are at the forefront of spiritual thought and experience. While each has something different to say, they all say it in a voice that you can hear.

Our books are designed to welcome you and then to engage, stimulate, and inspire. We judge our success not only by whether or not our books are beautiful and commercially successful, but by whether or not they make a difference in your life.